Original title:
A Taste of Sunshine

Copyright © 2025 Creative Arts Management OÜ
All rights reserved.

Author: Cassandra Whitaker
ISBN HARDBACK: 978-1-80586-316-8
ISBN PAPERBACK: 978-1-80586-788-3

Warm Emotions

On a sunny day, I wore my hat,
As bees buzzed around, and I chased a cat.
The ice cream melted, dripped down my chin,
I laughed so hard, it tickled my skin.

The pool was calling, splashes rang out,
I dove right in, but I landed on doubt.
My friends all giggled, I swam like a rock,
Sunshine's charm, it tickles the clock.

Radiant Footprints

Footprints in sand, a comical sight,
My flip-flops flipped, took off in delight.
I chased them down, through laughter we soared,
Sunshine and giggles, a perfect accord.

The seagulls squeaked as they swooped for fries,
I waved my arms, a funny disguise.
They took off laughing, my lunch was their prize,
Sunlight and humor shine bright in the skies.

Echoes of Warmth

The sun's rays danced, on the ground they played,
I tried to race them, but I quickly swayed.
Tripped on my shoes, oh what a scene,
Fell on the grass, felt like a queen.

A picnic spread out, with sandwiches stacked,
But squirrels had plans and quickly attacked.
They made off laughing with crumbs in their claws,
Chasing my snacks, they earned round of applause.

The Glow of Dusk

As the sun dipped low, we told silly tales,
Of pirates and treasure with wind in our sails.
Laughter erupted, a tickle-fest found,
With shadows that danced, oh joy did abound.

We roasted marshmallows, set them on fire,
My stick caught ablaze, I yelled, 'Not my desire!'
The glow of the dusk lit our smiles so wide,
In silly mishaps, together we glide.

Laughter in the Light

The sun spills gold on my cereal,

I laugh as I munch on my fruity cereal.
Kids think it's magic, I know the trick,
Silly glee in every crunchy click.

Bubbles are dancing, they tickle my chin,
Sunshine and giggles, let the fun begin!
The dog steals my lunch, what a furry thief,
Yet in this bright moment, I can't help but be chief.

Citrus Dreams

I dream in zest, with lemons galore,
Their tangy whispers, oh what a score!
Oranges juggle with giggles on high,
Citrus laughter sprouts wings and can fly.

Limes leap in napkins, sharp as a dart,
Pineapples dance, playing classical art.
Each squeeze is a chuckle, a tickle, a tease,
Sunshine in smoothies puts me at ease.

Dancing in Dawn's Embrace

The morning stretches and yawns a bright ray,
I dance with my slippers, come join the sway.
Toast on the counter starts doing the jig,
Coffee perks up, now that's a big gig!

Rays paint the skies, colors splash and swirl,
My cat pirouettes, oh what a whirl!
Chasing sunbeams, down the hall we dash,
In this golden hour, nothing can clash.

Honeyed Moments

In the breakfast room, honey drips sweet,
I toast to the day, oh what a treat!
Waffles and giggles, syrupy cheer,
Every bite bursts with joy, never fear.

Buzzing around is a bee full of glee,
Hoping for crumbs of this sweet jubilee.
Sticky-fingered grins, laughter my muse,
In honeyed moments, there's nothing to lose.

Sun-soaked Narratives

Oh, the sun spilled lemonade on my hat,
While squirrels danced, very much like that.
I tried to catch rays in a jar with a lid,
But they giggled and flew like a mischievous kid.

A pickle ran past with a glimmering grin,
It said, 'Chase me quick, let the fun begin!'
We tumbled through daisies, our laughter took flight,
In this sunny mischief, everything felt right.

Flavors of Paradise

The sun served ice cream, not a cloud in sight,
With sprinkles of joy dancing left and right.
A banana split laughed as it juggled shy,
While cherries and toppings joined in to fly.

We dipped our toes in a lemonade sea,
Where octopuses twirled in jubilee.
A fortune cookie whispered from a grape vine,
'Life's just a party, so let's sip the sunshine!'

Dawn's Gentle Kiss

When dawn crept in with a giggling breeze,
It tickled the flowers, 'Oh please, oh please!'
A toast with the robins, we sipped from the dew,
While pancakes flipped high in a sky painted blue.

The sun winked funny, like a playful chap,
I hid my cereal in a sunbeam's lap.
With syrupy dreams drizzled over my day,
Oh, how I danced in this silly ballet!

The Warmth of Tomorrow

On Tuesday, we dance with zest,
Chasing shadows, we jest.
Lemonade spills on our toes,
While giggles float in sun-kissed flows.

Bumblebees buzz like they know best,
As we nap on a cloud's soft crest.
With ice cream melting in our hands,
We make giggly, silly plans.

Citrus Dreams

Pineapple hats and orange shoes,
We waltz with a giggly muse.
Grapefruit boats on puddle seas,
We sail away in a sticky breeze.

Sunbeams tickle our funny bones,
As fruit flies make silly tones.
With every splash and joyful shout,
We're the best kind of silly scout.

Morning's Bold Brush

With toast that pops like fireworks,
We start the day with goofy quirks.
Peanut butter on our nose,
Oh, the laugh that surely grows!

Colors swirl in splendid cheer,
As breakfast dances, oh so near.
Cereal rainbows, what a view,
Each spoonful whispers funny too!

Honeyed Daydreams

In the garden, where bees do hum,
We chase each other, oh what fun!
Sticky fingers and sweetened cheer,
Every giggle is caught near.

Butterflies wear hats so bright,
Joining us in morning light.
With honey dripped on our faces wide,
We dream of snacks, oh, what a ride!

Sun-drenched Bliss

On a lazy day, the sun spills cheer,
With ice cream drips, it's clear, oh dear!
Squirrels dance, they make a fuss,
While I just giggle, melting like the fuss.

Grass stains on my favorite jeans,
Life's a circus, or so it seems.
Butterflies flaunt their silly tricks,
Catch them quick, before the kicks!

A sunbeam tickles my nose just right,
While shadows play, it's pure delight.
The sky's a canvas, wild and bright,
You'd think the world just loves to bite!

So let's embrace this sunny spree,
With lemonade laughs and goofy glee.
In this silly twist of nature's script,
I sip my drink and just let it rip!

Lively Reflections

Mirror, mirror, sunlit gleam,
My hat's too big, or so it seems.
Reflections bounce like bouncy balls,
I duck and dodge, I hear the calls.

A picnic spread with ants in tow,
They steal my sandwich, like it's a show.
What's that noise? A burst of sound,
Oh wait, it's just a friend, joyfully unbound!

Chasing shadows, laughing loud,
Sunshine makes us feel so proud.
With goofy grins and playful scowls,
We dance like only kids know how.

So here's to days of warm delight,
We chase the sun till falls the night.
With every giggle and silly cheer,
Life shines best when friends are near!

Bright Hues of Life

A rainbow's burst on pancakes bright,
Maple syrup takes a daring flight.
Cotton candy clouds up in the sky,
Only wish my worries could also fly.

Lemonade stands where kids collide,
With sticky fingers, we dance and slide.
A splash of joy in every joke,
As giggles float on a bubble cloak.

Whimsical suns with winking faces,
In the park, we claim our bases.
Kick the ball, watch it soar and spree,
Oh, how this wackiness sets us free!

So let's paint this day with glee,
Every shade of fun, come join the spree.
Together we'll splash in joy's delight,
Under the sun, everything feels right!

Fields of Gold

Golden fields where laughter grows,
I chase my hat as the wind blows.
Sunflowers wave like they've all won,
I trip and tumble, laughing, oh what fun!

Bunnies hop and giggle too,
They know the secrets we all pursue.
The grass tickles my feet, oh dear,
Where's the bug spray? I think it's near!

With kites that soar and squeals of bliss,
Let's capture this moment, I can't miss.
A picnic disaster, crumbs everywhere,
But who will mind? We're light as air!

In the fields of dreams and sunny sights,
We dance like stars on summer nights.
So let's embrace this playful twist,
With every chuckle, none can resist!

A Palette of Light

When lemons laugh with zest so bright,
The morning giggles, oh what a sight!
Orange peels dance and sway with glee,
While grapefruits hang like they're off a tree.

Butterflies paint with colors bold,
Tickling flowers that secretly scold.
Sunbeams tickle the edges of grass,
While bees in bow ties zip right past.

Rainbows blend as breakfast is served,
Fried egg sun round, it truly deserved!
Milkshakes swirl like the summer breeze,
While pancakes smile, doing as they please.

So come, take a bite of this playful feast,
Where every moment's a giggling beast.
With a sip of joy and a pinch of fun,
Life's a party under the playful sun!

Serenade of the Sun

Oh, sing me a tune from the blazing sky,
Where marshmallows melt and giggles fly.
The sun strums rays on a golden guitar,
While shadows peek out, all ready to spar.

Pineapples wear crowns, they rule the day,
With passionate dances, they lead the way.
Watermelons chuckle with every bite,
As ants twirl beneath, oh what a sight!

An umbrella shades a snail's slow groove,
While sunlight teases the breeze to move.
Lollipops spin like tops in the park,
Under sunny skies from dawn until dark.

So gather your friends, it's a musical cheer,
Where each note of laughter rings crystal clear.
With every beat, our hearts will race,
In this serenade, we find our place!

Embrace of the Horizon

At dusk, the horizon winks with delight,
Grinning clouds putting up a friendly fight.
Cotton candy skies, oh what a tease!
While giggling stars don their twinkling keys.

The sun dips low in a comedic bow,
Casting shadows that dance and wow.
Peanut butter clouds with jelly on top,
Play hide and seek, never wanting to stop.

Crickets start rapping in the twilight glow,
Grasshoppers join, putting on a show.
Lightning bugs blink like disco lights,
While moonwalks echo through playful nights.

In this embrace, laughter fills the air,
With whispers of joy, we dance without care.
A comedy sketch of colors and sounds,
Where happiness blooms and giggling abounds!

The Golden Hour

When the clock strikes fun, it's the golden hour,
Bananas peel off laughter, that's their power.
With giggling skies and candy fluff dreams,
Marshmallows bounce like sunlight beams.

Sipping on sunshine from a coconut cup,
Where jellybeans rain and never give up.
Rainbow sprinkles sprinkle the jokes on the side,
While gummy bears race with sprightly pride.

Skateboards zoom past, a colorful blur,
As cupcake clouds tumble in a sweet whirr.
Sandcastles giggle as tides come to play,
In the joy of the moment, we all sway.

So grab your laughter and dance in the light,
In this golden hour, everything feels right.
With smiles and giggles, we'll sing out loud,
Celebrating life, oh we're so proud!

Vibrant Associates

When lemons bring laughter to our day,
And tangerines dance in a funny way.
My friends are the zest, full of cheer,
They make sun rays seem so near.

We roast marshmallows on sunbeams bright,
And giggle at ducks in silly flight.
A pineapple hat atop my head,
Fruit fashion shows are where we tread.

Their jokes grow like daisies in spring,
We laugh so loud, our hearts take wing.
Picking daisies without a care,
And tickling clouds up in the air.

So let's stroll where the rays play
And turn drab moments into a cabaret.
With vibrant pals and bright, quirky quirks,
Every mundane task becomes our perks.

Sundrenched Letters

I sent a postcard full of smiles,
To a friend who lives by the miles.
"I've found a sunbeam," I wrote with glee,
"It's wearing shades, come join me!"

They replied with a sketch of a cat in a tie,
Sipping lemonade with a laugh and a sigh.
"Let's plan a trip to the land of delight,
Where sunshine never takes flight!"

Each letter drips with comic flair,
Sent with sunshine and a touch of air.
Envelopes stuffed with silly notes,
And doodles of goats wearing coats!

So here we plot our merry escapade,
With sun's golden rays, plans are laid.
We'll collect giggles in a jar,
And ship them back from afar!

Glowing Pathways

We ventured forth on golden tracks,
With squirrels giggling at our backs.
Paths of laughter laid before,
With sunshine tickling us at the core.

Each step we took, the world grew bright,
Doing the cha-cha, what a sight!
Side-stepping puddles with a splash,
As sunlight joined in our funny bash.

We spotted fairies playing chess,
Wearing hats that were quite the mess.
"Care for a game?" one fairy said,
While munching on toast that I had spread.

With glowing paths and shoes of twirl,
Every step feels like a whirl.
In each giggle, the world ignites,
Bright and cheerful in endless flights!

Cherished Illuminations

In the kitchen, chaos blooms,
With toasters popping, filling rooms.
We bake a cake with frosting bright,
While dog in sunglasses steals the light.

A blender whirls like a merry whirlpool,
Mixing laughter as a family rule.
The secret recipe? A wink or two,
And silly faces to brighten the view.

We gather 'round as the cake combines,
With sprinkles dancing like happy signs.
"Who needs forks?" someone shouts with glee,
"We'll dive right in, just you and me!"

Each bite is a giggle, every crumb shared,
Moments so silly, our hearts declared.
In the glow of love and laughter's embrace,
A party of joy, our sunny space!

Warmth on the Breeze

The sun spills laughter, full of cheer,
Tickles your nose, it's almost near.
Birds in shades of yellow socks,
Dance on rooftops, they're such jocks.

Breezes blow like playful jesters,
Chasing hats, those crafty testers.
A squirrel wearing shades zooms by,
While clouds are just popcorn in the sky.

Serenade of Sunbeams

Sunbeams play hide and seek, my friend,
Chasing shadows, around each bend.
The light winks bright, a silly tease,
Making me laugh with such great ease.

A butterfly dons a tiny hat,
Flitting by like a jazzy cat.
"Catch me if you can!" it flares,
While the flowers are throwing their chairs.

Radiance in the Air

The radiance tickles my silly nose,
Warming giggles from feet to toes.
It's a radiant show, come take a seat,
The daisies are dancing, oh what a feat!

A duck in sunglasses waddles along,
Quacking out notes to a sunny song.
Through puddles of laughter, the sun does glide,
While ants march by, full of pride.

Embrace of Daybreak

Daybreak hugs me, a bright embrace,
Waking up my sleepy face.
The rooster has a morning grin,
As he crows out, "Let the fun begin!"

Pancakes do a little twirl,
While syrup's ready to dance and swirl.
With sunshine pancakes stacked so high,
Even the ants give it a try!

Festival of Light

Dancing shadows, waltzing bright,
Candles flicker, what a sight!
Jellybeans toss in air,
Who knew sweets would dance with flair?

Glow sticks waving, kids outsmart,
A glowworm party? Now that's art!
Balloon animals take a bow,
What a scene, oh, wow, wow, wow!

Warmth in the Void

In winter chill, a cat in shades,
Sipping cocoa, while it parades.
Marshmallows bounce, looking spry,
Hot chocolate dreams, oh me, oh my!

Snowflakes giggle, do a twirl,
Frosty flakes with a swirl and whirl.
A snowman grinning, carrot nose,
With a scarf that flutters as he goes!

The Glint of Joy

Chasing bubbles in the air,
Giggling kids with sparkly hair.
Silly faces, ice cream bliss,
Mismatched socks, how could you miss?

Puppies prancing, tails up high,
Jumping through puddles, oh my, oh my!
With every splash, laughter grows,
Who knew fun could pay in prose?

Mirthful Daze

With a pie faced first in line,
Laughter erupts, feeling divine.
Squirrels plotting sneaky raids,
While humans dance in jubilee parades.

Tickle fights turn into races,
Silly hats hide grinning faces.
A game of tag in loading carts,
Let's keep the laughter, it warms our hearts!

Bright Whimsy

Lemonade spills on the floor,
Cats chase shadows, wanting more.
Ice cream drips down my chin,
Giggles erupt, let the fun begin.

Balloons float high in the air,
Tangled in trees, without a care.
Silly hats on every head,
Who knew summer's so wild? I'm fed!

Grass stains on knees, oh what a sight,
Fireflies dance in the twilight.
Dancing barefoot, what a delight,
As the stars twinkle, oh so bright.

Summer's Embrace

Sunglasses perched on my nose,
Riding bikes, it's quite a pose.
Flip-flops slapping, hear the sound,
Who knew fun could be so profound?

Watermelon juice on my shirt,
A bee buzzes, oh what a flirt.
Splashing in puddles, laughter's a must,
In summer's joy we all trust.

Kites soaring high, they take flight,
Boys challenging girls, what a sight!
Sandcastles built with giggles and cheer,
Summer's here, let's all yell "Yippee!"

Golden Embrace

Sunshine giggles through the trees,
Chasing shadows with the breeze.
Picnic blankets spread with treats,
Ants march in line, oh what feats!

Popsicles melting, sticky sweet,
Everyone's dancing, can't miss a beat.
A squirrel sneaks off with our snack,
Yelling, "Hey you, bring that back!"

Jumpsuits donned, looking quite fly,
We paint the sky, oh my, oh my!
Geysers of laughter, bubbles of glee,
Summer days are pure jubilee.

Rays of Joy

Sunbeams tickle my cheek, oh bliss,
Playing tag, what a hit or miss.
Jumping waves, splashing about,
Our raucous laughter, a jubilant shout!

Barbecue smoke fills the air,
Misdirected marshmallows, beware!
Who made s'mores? A gooey sight,
Chasing fireflies into the night.

Silly contests, who can balance?
Wobbling hats—a summer dance!
Tickle fights under the sun,
In this sunshine, we all have fun.

Joyful Sunrays

The sun pours out like lemonade,
Bright beams dance in a sneak parade.
Up to mischief, they tickle toes,
Chasing shadows where no one goes.

Giggling clouds lend a fluffy touch,
Swinging low, they don't care much.
Sunbeams wiggle, oh what a sight,
Playing tag with bees in flight.

With each glare, the cheeky rays,
Pretend to nap, then jump and play.
Joking with the leaves and grass,
Bouncing around like joyous brass.

Laughing flowers twist and bend,
Under the heat, they wiggle, blend.
Nature's laughter fills the scene,
A sunny prankster's happy dream.

Sweetness in the Glow

Golden drizzles on my face,
Sticky fingers, a sugar race.
The sun's been baking every treat,
Warm cookies for the sunny street.

Lemonade spills, so tart and bright,
Giggles echo with pure delight.
Sweet sunshine melts on the sand,
Making every moment grand.

Cotton candy clouds float by,
As kids chase bubbles to the sky.
Sunshine sprinkles some silly fun,
Lemon lollipops, oh how they run!

Fluffy pancakes rise like dough,
Dancing on plates with a golden glow.
Each bite brings a laugh, a cheer,
As sweetness spreads from ear to ear.

Sunlit Silhouettes

Shadows stretch, a funny sight,
Dancing tall in the warm daylight.
Silly shapes wave and sway,
Playing games until end of day.

Birds wear hats made of the sun,
Laughing loudly as they run.
Caught in rays of laughter bright,
Their joyous tunes take lofty flight.

Sunlit figures prance about,
Chasing squirrels, there's no doubt.
A cheeky breeze twirls the leaves,
Mocking each one, oh what a tease!

But when the daylight starts to fade,
Silly shapes in the grass invade.
Whispered giggles in the dusk,
As night tells tales of sun and husk.

Blossoms of Radiance

Bright blooms pop like joyful pranks,
Waving cheer with their zany flanks.
Each petal is a painted joke,
Spreading giggles with each poke.

Sunflower hats and rosy cheeks,
Whirling colors, so unique.
A bouquet of mischief blooms,
Spilling laughter through the rooms.

Pollen dances, a fuzzy friend,
Joking with bees, they twist and bend.
Each wildflower winks with glee,
In the bright sun, wild and free.

With every petal's painted grin,
Joyful chaos starts to spin.
The world in colors, bright and bold,
A funny garden waiting to unfold.

Gentle Radiance

A bright yellow cat, sunbathing sprawled,
Woke up with a stretch and instantly appalled.
His spot is now gone, taken by shade,
He plotted revenge in a sunbeam parade.

Birds in the trees, they chatter and cheer,
While squirrels scamper, 'It's peanut time, dear!'
They dance in confusion, prancing with glee,
As the sun takes a break, sipping iced herbal tea.

A dog appears next, with a wag of his tail,
Stealing the scene like a canine whale.
He somersaults hard, lands right on the grass,
Spreading his joy, what a funny little rascal!

Under the warm glow, we all share a laugh,
A parade of oddities, perfect in half.
With giggles and snorts, the day feels so bright,
In this gentle radiance, we bask in delight.

The Sunshine Within

A cucumber grins, in the fridge he's the king,
He jokes with a carrot about the joys they bring.
"I'm crisp and I'm cool, I'm the life of the party!"
Replies the poor carrot, "Man, you're so hearty!"

Tomatoes roll in, feeling bold and spry,
"Let's salsa it up—why not give it a try?"
In a blender they giggle, all chopped into bits,
'Cause nothing says fun like a fruit salad blitz!

A quirky potato, with a hat made of foil,
Prances about, rearranging the soil.
He shouts, "I'm the star of this garden revue!
With a side of my friends, we're serving something new!"

As sunlight pours down, the laughter ignites,
In the kitchen parade, everyone delights.
With whispers of joy in this veggie delight,
The sunshine within makes everything right.

Dancing on Sunbeams

A little bug winks, as he takes to the floor,
He kicks up his heels and starts to explore.
"Look here, I've found the best light for my groove!"
With a flick of his wings, he begins to move.

Next comes a snail, moving slow but precise,
With a shell that's quite shiny, oh so nice!
He grooves to the rhythm, his trail leaves a shine,
As he slinks to the music, 'This is my time!'

A ladybug joins, tapping her spots,
"Let's boogie on petals; forget all our knots!"
With flowers as partners, they whirl and they spin,
In this comical dance, every laugh wears a grin.

When the sun starts to dip, they each take a bow,
"A round of applause! What a show! Take a bow!"
They giggle and laugh, the day's been so bright,
Dancing on sunbeams, into the night.

Illumination of the Heart

A bright-eyed squirrel, with a nut like a crown,
Claims he's the jester, funking around town.
He juggles his treasures, a marvelous feat,
But oops, there it goes—a slippery treat!

A duck quacks in, with a style so divine,
"Join in my parade, let's all drink some wine!"
With feathers a-fluff, they march through the park,
Holding their heads high, with a quack and a spark.

An old tortoise winks, says, "I'm slow, but I shine,
With wisdom and jokes, let the laughter align!"
And the grass giggles back, tickled by the sun,
In this silly tableau, all worry is done.

As the day wraps in light, they share one last cheer,
"Here's to the warmth; let's spread all the cheer!"
With a wink and a nudge, they part with delight,
In the illumination of the heart, all feels right.

Mirth in the Meadow

In the field where daisies dance,
Bumblebees wear tiny pants.
Grasshoppers hop with silly pride,
Chasing clouds, they glide and slide.

A squirrel in shades takes a ride,
On a pig's back, oh what a stride!
Laughter echoes, winds take a peek,
Nature's parties, wild and chic.

Cows hold court with a royal moo,
While chickens plot to join the crew.
The sun winks down with golden cheer,
In this meadow, fun is near!

Sing and dance, let worries flee,
Join the frolic, wild and free.
With laughter bright like dandelion,
In the meadow, joy's a lion.

Cherished Flare

A sunbeam slips through leafy trees,
Tickling toes and swaying knees.
Butterflies in tutus prance,
While rabbits join the light-hearted dance.

Jellybeans rain down from above,
Popping candy, sweet like love.
A ladybug wears a tiny crown,
With fruit punch flowing all around.

Sunflowers wave with a bright "hello!"
While ants promote their summer show.
Lemonade stands pop up everywhere,
Sipping joy becomes a dare.

Dancing shadows, giggles shared,
In this glow, no one is spared.
With cherished flare, we toast and cheer,
As laughter sparkles, far and near.

Vivid Embrace

In the park, bright colors burst,
While squirrels line up to thirst.
A picnic spread with goodies galore,
Cheetahs chase sandwiches, oh what a score!

Jesters in jello wiggle and sway,
Telling jokes in a silly way.
Dancing in circles, round and round,
As giggles bubble from the ground.

Kites fly high, with tails so long,
While frogs croak out their ribbit song.
Joy bounces like a bouncing ball,
In vivid embrace, we laugh and sprawl.

Handstands and cartwheels rule the scene,
As shadows dance, so fresh and clean.
With every twist, a new surprise,
In this day, mirth never dies.

Sunlit Pathways

On sunlit paths, we prance and hop,
With giggles echoing, we can't stop.
Lemon trees wear hats of zest,
While we parade in a silly quest.

Puppies twirl in a merry race,
Chasing butterflies, quickening pace.
Postcards of laughter flutter around,
As sunshine tickles the happy ground.

Berries burst with jammy delight,
As raccoons dance under twilight.
Every smile is a precious gem,
In this bright world, we are all ahem!

Balloons set sail on a breezy day,
With whispers of joy that lead the way.
On sunlit pathways, fun abounds,
As we laugh out loud, in silly rounds.

Serene Sunrises

The rooster crows, all bright and bold,
Coffee spills, like tales retold.
Pajamas dance on hasty feet,
As we race for breakfast treats.

Muffins tumble, butter flies,
Syrup drips from smiling pies.
Giggling under morning's cheer,
Where all is light and milk may smear.

A dog in shades, all cool and spry,
Chasing shadows, oh my, oh my!
Socks mismatched, a fashion sin,
In this morning, joy's a win!

With sunlight streaking through the blinds,
We dance around like silly finds.
For in this glow, we can't be serious,
A sunrise laugh feels oh-so-mysterious.

The Glow of Laughter

A giggle here, a chuckle there,
Laughter bubbles in the air.
The sun beams down, a playful tease,
In this moment, hearts feel at ease.

Tickles from the rays above,
Encourage us to dance and shove.
We bump, we trip, we roll around,
Joy's not lost, but rather found!

Hats askew, our hair a mess,
Moments like these, we must confess.
We write our stories, wild and bright,
In laughter's glow, we find our light.

Morning whispers, 'Join the fun!',
Our hearts beat fast; we've just begun!
Amidst the giggles, shine anew,
In this glow, dreams come in two.

Morning Light

The sun unfurls, a golden sheet,
Covered in crumbs from last night's treat.
The toaster pops, a dance in dawn,
Fry the bacon, till it's brown!

The cat's on guard with sleepy eyes,
While toast avoids the pop-up surprise.
Jams and jellies have a spat,
And breakfast turns into a chat.

Socks on the ceiling, cushions in the air,
Who knew mornings could be so rare?
With peanut butter dreams in flight,
Our hearts are filled with morning light.

In this chaos, we find our way,
With laughter leading us astray.
Every sip of coffee we take,
In morning light, we giggle awake.

Evening Dreams

The day departs, the sun retreats,
As shadows play in warm evenings' feats.
The streetlamps glow, a buzzing hum,
While crickets chirp, a gentle drum.

With ice cream drips and giggles loud,
We twirl in moonlight, feeling proud.
Under starlit skies, we dream and scheme,
In the twilight, everything's a meme!

Couch cushions launched in the heat of night,
Pillow fights and feathery flight.
The world outside, a sleepy scene,
While we concoct our wildest dream.

And though the day will start anew,
We dance in dreams, just me and you.
In every silly, starry beam,
We find our laughter in the dream.

Sweetness in the Air

With cupcakes frosted, smiles abound,
Sweetness dances all around.
Lemonade stands on every street,
In every corner, friends we greet.

A cherry bomb of giggles bursts,
Noses sticky, it's the worst!
But joy's our flavor mixed so well,
In ice cream dreams, we laugh and yell.

Pies that wobble, laughter spills,
On our cheeks, the sugar thrills.
From candy clouds and cookie rain,
Every joke's a sweet refrain!

So grab a friend, don't think twice,
In this sweetness, life feels nice!
With every flavor, every cheer,
We taste the joy that's always near.

Honeyed Horizons

Golden rays dance on my toast,
Butterflies gossip, they like to boast.
Jam spills over, what a sticky mess,
Sweetness abounds, it's anyone's guess.

The sun's a comedian, shining so bright,
Tickling the trees, what a silly sight.
Lemonade jokes pour from every glass,
Sipping on laughter, let the good times pass.

With every giggle, the clouds start to grin,
Even the daisies are in on the chin.
Giggling shadows waltz on the grass,
Dancing together as moments amass.

The world feels like candy wrapped up in cheer,
Beneath the sun's laughter, let's all just steer.
Grab your glasses, you've nothing to lose,
In this bright frolic, it's just pure muse.

Sunlit Tendrils

The sun peeks through, with tickles and tease,
Frolicking colors like playful bees.
Each beam a tickle, a warm gentle nudge,
Turning grumpy faces with its sunny grudge.

A flip-flop fiasco, lost in the lawn,
Hats blown away, they're a comical spawn.
The squirrels start chattering, plotting their heist,
Gathering treasures, being quite nice!

Lemon treats dance with the breezy delight,
Whispers of sunshine make everything bright.
What a ruckus, a delightful parade,
Of ice cream shenanigans in the shade.

With each burst of laughter that spills all around,
The flowers are chuckling, and joy is profound.
Grab a giggle, let the good vibes stick,
In this sunlit comedy, we've got the trick!

Kisses from Above

The sun slurps down like a fizzy drink,
Poking cheeks rosy, making folks wink.
Puddles of joy, where shadows play hide,
Jumping in laughter, let's take a ride!

Clouds fluff up like whipped cream delight,
A playful pastry in the splendor of light.
Bubbles of giggles float up to the sky,
Chasing the sunbeams, just let 'em fly!

Each ray throws jokes with a warm little sigh,
Sun-kissed moments stretch long like the sky.
Cool breezes dance, like socks on the grass,
Messy and merry, let the moments amass.

So let's toast to the magic that brightens our day,
Kisses from above help us laugh and play.
Catch those rays that twinkle like sparks,
In this quirky sitcom, we dance till it larks.

Harvesting Light

Bananas chuckle on the fruit stand display,
Orange giggles brightening up the day.
Mangoes flirt with the ones next in line,
Jokingly swaying like they're sipping wine.

The sun spills nectar like honeyed delight,
Tickling the tomatoes, oh what a sight!
Carrot capers sprout out of their place,
Saying, "Come dance, join our goofy chase!"

Each laugh echoes, bouncing off trees,
Zucchinis rolling, they can't help but tease.
Lettuce leaf turns with a marvelous grin,
Making salad jokes in the bright, bright din.

Grab your baskets, let's gather the cheer,
In this joyful harvest, let's spread some cheer.
For every sunbeam that brightens our plight,
Are bites of laughter, we're harvesting light.

Luminous Echoes

A lemon fell right from a tree,
It bounced and rolled, oh what a spree!
A squirrel caught it, thought it was gold,
He danced around, so brave and bold.

A duck quacked loud, just to complain,
'Why can't I find a snack this sane?'
But nearby, bees buzzed with delight,
Sharing their honey, oh what a sight!

The sun peeked through a fluffy cloud,
Telling all creatures to laugh out loud.
The turtles jumped, the rabbits skedaddled,
Chasing bright beams, they giggled and rattled.

A rainbow formed after a light rain,
Frogs in tuxedos started their train.
While all the kids waved with glee,
"Best day ever!" they shouted with plea!

Daydreams Under Bright Skies

Under the sun, a picnic spread,
The ants had plans, a fine buffet ahead.
While sandwiches wiggled, pretzels would dance,
A soup made of sunshine? They'd give it a chance!

A dog in shades lounged on a mat,
Chasing a butterfly, imagine that!
The owner sighed, "Stop being so lazy!"
But the pup just snored, looking all hazy.

Crackers and cheese rolled down the hill,
Where rabbits and raccoons began their thrill.
They formed a band, with spoons and a pan,
Playing sunshine tunes like a music fan.

As clouds puffed up like cotton candy,
Kids chased the breeze, feeling quite dandy.
"Oh look!" they yelled, in a fit of joy,
"Even the sun's playing our favorite toy!"

Glimmers of Bliss

A jellybean slid off the table,
Bouncing like mad, it felt so able!
It rolled and jumped in a silly chase,
With giggles and chuckles, it found its place.

The sunbeam tickled a sleeping cat,
Who woke with a stretch and a soft little spat.
It chased shadows with all of its flair,
Turning the garden into a fair!

Crayons got together for a art show,
Sunshine yellow stole the whole glow.
They drew bright flowers, a dancing bee,
And a smiling sun sipping warm tea!

Amidst all the fun, a butterfly sneezed,
The world erupted, laughter increased.
Jellybeans danced, while colors blended,
In a whirl of joy, the day never ended!

Honey Drops in the Afternoon

A pickle in a jar opened up wide,
With a loud pop, it burst out with pride!
It juggled some carbs, with onions in tow,
Causing a ruckus at the lunch show.

Honey dripped from a hive on the tree,
Bees wearing goggles, buzzing with glee.
They coated the picnic with sunshine sweet,
While ants brought the cake for a tasty treat.

A squirrel brought forks, the fun was complete,
Together they feasted, no one skipped a beat.
Laughter rose high, under skies so blue,
As they toasted with lemonade, all smiles anew.

And just when they thought it was winding down,
A bee led a dance, spinning round and round.
The sun giggled loud, casting its rays,
As nature joined in for the best of days!

Flickers of Radiance

In a jar, I caught a ray,
Thought I'd drink it, come what may.
A sip of laughter, bright and bold,
My face turned warm, a sight to behold.

With every beam, I feel so spry,
Chasing shadows that wave goodbye.
Sunshine tickles my funny bone,
Even the clouds laugh, not alone.

I tried to bake a sunny pie,
But burnt it all, oh my, oh my!
The smell was sweet, the taste was dire,
Yet still I danced, like I was fire.

So grab your shades, let's run outside,
We'll boogie like we're on a ride.
With every chuckle, the day is won,
Flickers of joy, bright as the sun.

Glistening Horizons

The dawn breaks with a wink and grin,
Chasing away sleep's silly din.
A bird flies by, in a top hat too,
Singing tunes of the jolly crew.

Horizons gleam with a golden hue,
Glimmers of joy, a playful view.
I tripped on air, fell flat on grass,
Laughed so hard, I lost my class.

Neighbors shout, "What's all this cheer?"
I wave my arms and sip my beer.
Every glance at the sun's bright jest,
Cracks a smile, it's all for the best.

So let's embrace this silly spree,
With clouds that dance, so wild and free.
In every giggle and goofy twist,
Glistening moments we can't resist.

Sunbeam Serenade

A beam of light with a silly grin,
Swaying and dancing, oh where to begin?
I followed it down a rabbit hole,
And ended up in a candle's role.

The sun sang sweetly, off-key, of course,
Tapping its rays like a merry horse.
Bouncing and laughing with glee galore,
Each note a tickle, who could ask for more?

I joined the tune, with pots and pans,
Rattling rhythms, silly dance plans.
The squirrels joined in, a colorful crew,
Twisting their tails, like they always do.

With sunlight swirling all around,
I belly-laughed, fell hard to the ground.
In this serenade that brings such fun,
Every moment shines, I won't be done!

Melodies of the Dawn

Morning whispers in a cheeky tone,
Tickling toes while I bumble alone.
Pancakes flip with a playful flair,
Laughter spills over like syrup in air.

Birds compete in a silly race,
Chirping their songs, what a loud place!
I clap my hands, join their parade,
Who knew waking up could be this grade?

The coffee's brewing a punchy dance,
A frothy mustache—oh, what a chance!
With each sip, I chuckle and sway,
Melodies bounce me into the day.

So let the dawn play its funny part,
With each bright note, it warms the heart.
In every giggle that breaks the morn,
Melodies of joy, forever reborn.

Cornflower Days

The sky is blue, like grandma's hat,
The sun's a big old smiling cat.
Flipping pancakes from the grill,
They land on roofs, what a thrill!

Silly birds dance with their feet,
While squirrels argue over a treat.
Jumping puddles, just for kicks,
Our laughter's scattered like confetti sticks.

Butterflies wear boots and hats,
While ants hold parades with their chitchats.
Every corner filled with cheer,
Who knew sunshine could be so dear?

Cornflower days, they whiz and zoom,
Like toddlers racing round the room.
With lemonade by the swinging door,
We'll dance like shadows, always wanting more.

Splendor in the Air

The clouds are puffs of sugary fluff,
With squeaky ducks saying, "That's enough!"
Sunscreen smudged across my nose,
A sunburn forming in funny rows.

Ice cream drips down my new white shirt,
Mom yells, "Why don't you just flirt?"
With sticky fingers and giggly toes,
We chase the breeze wherever it goes.

A kite's a fish that swims so high,
Shouting, "Catch me if you can, I fly!"
We tumble in grass, we crawl and roll,
In this comedy, we take the toll.

The splendor dances and takes a peek,
As laughter bubbles, cheek to cheek.
Funny moments sprinkled bright,
In golden rays, our hearts take flight.

Tapestry of Rays

A tapestry sewn with wild delight,
Bringing butterflies to the family sight.
Frisbees glide like flying pies,
While grandpa tells his big fish lies.

The picnic spread, a feast of fun,
Where ants march like soldiers on the run.
Sandwiches laugh; one ran away,
"Come back!" we yell, "Don't disobey!"

Neighbors squawk, watering their yards,
While kids craft ketchup mustard guards.
Our little kingdom, a castle grand,
With pickle flags and jellybeans on hand.

Rays job like jesters in a show,
Spinning tales of where they'd go.
In this zany patch, we find our way,
Creating laughter in each sunny ray.

Lucent Journeys

In bubbles popping on the lawn,
We chase the light from dusk till dawn.
Each step a giggle, slippery slips,
Like jellybeans on happy trips.

Socks mismatched, oh what a sight!
They dance around in pure delight.
We ride our bikes like space cadets,
Passing by clowns and singing pets.

A treasure map drawn with crayon dreams,
Leading to places where laughter gleams.
With pizza slices as our guide,
Adventure awaits on this joyful ride.

So here's to trips that twirl and spin,
To all the places we might begin.
The sun may set, but fear not the night,
For tomorrow we'll chase that golden light.

Glimmers of Warmth

In the fridge, my juice conspired,
To taste like lemons, I'd admired.
But poured it out, oh what a mess!
Turns out it's pickles, I confess.

Sunbaked bread on a summer stand,
Danced away with a laugh so grand.
Butter slid with a wink and grin,
A sliding game I can't quite win.

My hat flew off on the breeze so sly,
Chasing it down, I thought I might cry.
But it landed soft on a passing pup,
Who wore it proud, like a fancy cup.

Sunshine tickled my toes, oh dear,
All the ants decided to cheer.
I danced away, they chased in line,
A marching band, I made them pine!

Brightened Souls

Giddy glow from a popsicle treat,
Melting quickly, oh what a feat!
Dripped on my shoe, now it's a spree,
Sticky adventures, just wait and see!

Sipping soda, a fizzy delight,
Bubbles popped with a wink in sight.
Then one jumped right in my nose,
Now I'm sneezing, and that's how it goes!

My friend wore shorts with colors so bright,
Blinded the sun, oh what a sight!
We giggled loud, a laughter parade,
Fashion faux pas, but love never fades.

Frolicking ducks tried to steal my fries,
They quacked at me with beady eyes.
Chased them off, but what a delight,
Even ducks want a taste of the bright!

Reflections of Day

Mirror, mirror, on the wall,
Why does my hair look like a ball?
The sun beams down with quirky rays,
And all my plans just wander away!

A lemonade stand, oh what a dream,
Except for bees that buzz and beam.
They wanted sips, but I was quick,
With a swat and a laugh, I did a trick!

Picnic blankets in disarray,
Sandwiches flying, come what may!
We played tag with runaway cake,
Hoping it's frosting, not a mistake!

A kite got tangled with grandma's hair,
She giggled back with plenty of flair.
So we tossed it high with a big cheer,
Just a sunny day with friends so near!

Dappled Dreams

In the garden, a squirrel took flight,
With my snack, he dashed out of sight.
I gave chase, laughed at his spree,
He stopped for a nut, but not for me!

Bubbles floated, a whimsical scene,
Popped 'em all—what a silly routine!
Now soap's on the grass, a slippery spot,
Fell with a giggle, oh what a lot!

A twirl in the sun, my skirt took a leap,
Caught in a gust, my secrets to keep.
Down the path with a shimmy and spin,
Dance of the daisies, let the fun begin!

Lost my shades in a wind-whipped hustle,
They flew away, what a funny tussle!
Now I squint like a pirate at sea,
Searching for sunshine and giggles with glee!

Warmth Between the Pages

A book dropped on the floor,
Pancakes flying out the door.
The cat lies sprawled, it's true,
Reading my mind like a shrew.

Sunshine spills on every scene,
Crumbs mysteriously unseen.
Whispers of tales wrapped in bread,
Who knew my pb&j could spread?

Laughter hides between each line,
A coffee cup, a splash of dine.
Bookmarks waving like a flag,
In the fridge, I found my brag.

But as the sunlight finds its way,
Stray thoughts dance and bounce and play.
Maybe pancakes have a say,
In the tales that brats betray!

Saffron Skies

The sky is dressed in shades of gold,
Like buttered popcorn, bright and bold.
I wore my sunglasses on a whim,
But now I find them looking dim.

A bird flew by with sass and cheer,
Dove straight down, took off my ear!
A tiny sun that made me squeal,
Cracked a joke with zest like a meal.

A cloud pretends to hide away,
Refuses to join the light ballet.
It tumbles 'round, won't take a cue,
Like uncle Joe at the BBQ!

I wave goodbye to all that's gray,
The saffron skies just want to play.
With laughter tickling every nook,
I read long verses from a cookbook!

Chasing Daylight

In the morning sun, I raced my shoes,
They squeaked and stalled, oh what a ruse!
Chasing after a warming glow,
Tripped on my own toe, oh no!

The shadows giggled, gave a shout,
They popped right out, said, "Let's hang out!"
Caught between the flip-flops' dance,
Chasing dreams that lead to chance.

A squirrel stole my plans in jest,
He scampered off, a fuzzy pest.
While I reek of sunblock's delight,
He nabbed my sandwich — quite the sight!

As daylight winks, I grumble slightly,
But I can't help but smile brightly.
I'll chase the sun, the sky's my quest,
And let the squirrel live as my guest!

Joy in the Shadows

In corners where the sunlight bends,
The shadows whisper, making friends.
A broomstick player with a hat,
Twirls 'round a spoon; imagine that!

Giggles hide behind the couch,
While toast pops high, I hear a ouch!
The cat leaps in with graceful flair,
Knocking down joy, and leaving air!

Lemons roll like laughter on tiles,
Statues smirk with cheesy smiles.
Every nook is a playful den,
Where sunshine laughs again and again.

So come out, join this silly dance,
Where shadows plot a secret chance.
Amidst this sunny, quirky sprawl,
The warmth of fun can win it all!

Light-Filled Reveries

In a jar, I found some glee,
Packed it up with lemon tea.
Tasted sweetness in a grin,
Sipped too fast, and now I'm spin!

Clouds were laughing, what a sight,
Turned my frown to pure delight.
Chased by shadows, my feet dance,
Tripped on joy, lost in a trance.

Sunbeams wiggle in the air,
Twisting curls and tousled hair.
Wrapped in warmth, I feel so spry,
Yet my sandwich just flew by!

Daisies giggle, they won't stop,
Winking at me from the crop.
In this world, I take my shot,
Finding fun in every blot.

Skies of Gold

Glittering clouds tease my head,
Bouncing dreams like jelly spread.
Jumping jacks on sunny beams,
Wiggly worms on candy streams.

Butterflies fling jokes around,
While I chase them on the ground.
Grins and giggles fill the air,
Wishing I had wings to share!

Pickles dancing on the roof,
Singing songs that make me goof.
Cucumbers dressed as balls of flair,
Have a party, why not dare?

As the sky paints shades of cheer,
Silly shadows draw me near.
At the picnic, ants parade,
Hoping none of them get made!

Sunshine Serenade

Balloons bouncing off the ground,
Squeaky laughter all around.
Playing tag with silly birds,
Chasing dreams, avoiding herds.

In a sunlit crowded park,
Jumping high, oh! What a lark!
Cookies dance across the field,
Only to be quickly sealed.

While I juggle dreams and pie,
Watch my sandwich touch the sky.
Bubbly giggles fill the scene,
Life's a joke, a madcap gleam.

Rainbows skip and twirl about,
Giving me a little shout.
Join the fun; let's run and play,
In this sunshine, every day!

Warm Hues of Happiness

In my pocket, sunshine sits,
Twirling round with giggly fits.
Wiggly worms wear tiny hats,
Skip and smile, oh! Fancy cats.

Lemon trees hum silly tunes,
While the sun draws happy moons.
Dancing leaves and honey bees,
All unite with playful ease.

Funny hats upon my head,
Cooking dreams like toasted bread.
With a wink, the sun agrees,
To join me in my playful tease.

Silly shadows, shadows long,
Start a chorus, sing along.
In this world of twinkling hues,
Every moment, laughter stews.

Twilight's Soft Caress

The sun slips down with a grin,
Whispers of laughter on its chin.
Grass tickles toes, all in a race,
Chasing shadows, oh what a place!

Fireflies dance in a dizzy swirl,
While pets leap high, giving a twirl.
Neighbors chuckle, such silly sights,
As kids break pencils in paper fights.

Old dogs snooze by the garden's edge,
While squirrels plot, each sneaky pledge.
What's the matter? Did they overhear?
The sound of joy, echoing near!

Moonrise brings a cool delight,
Funny faces in the fading light.
So let's toast to each silly thing,
With twilight's soft caress, we sing!

Sunlit Hopes

Sunshine spills like butter on toast,
Everything's brighter, let's all boast!
With lemonade smiles and hats too big,
We dance 'round the yard doing a jig!

Clouds peek down, their faces hide,
While we chase rainbows, full of pride.
A picnic's planned, with ants in line,
Trying to claim that sandwich of mine!

Fruits in bowls all start to play,
Bananas whisper, 'Give us today!'
Jellybeans bounce, plotting their scheme,
To create the craziest ice cream dream!

Laughter weaves through the summer air,
Caught in the moment, without a care.
Sunlit hopes dance on the breeze,
With goofy giggles, we're always at ease.

Sunkissed Horizons

A horizon painted with purple haze,
Silly suns pop with colorful rays.
A kite gets stuck on the neighbor's roof,
As laughter echoes, oh what a goof!

Beach balls roll like happy thoughts,
While seagulls plot, stealing our snacks.
Sunhats tumble, in a game of chase,
Giggling, we race with such silly grace!

Waves crash down with a splashy cheer,
"Who needs clothes?" someone asks near.
The sun laughs low, its rays like a tease,
While we make castles with wobbly knees!

With skies bright blue, we'll never stop,
At dusk, we'll dance till we drop.
Sunkissed horizons share their fun,
With giggles and joy, we always run!

Afternoon Reveries

The clock ticks slow, oh what a sight,
Afternoon dreams in the warm daylight.
Cats doze off, on windowsills wide,
While kids play tag, their joy can't hide!

Bubblegum giggles, oh what a sound,
A parade of laughter from all around.
A dog in sunglasses, strutting with flair,
Chasing its tail without a care!

Fruit flies hover, making their rounds,
While lemonade spills on the churn of sounds.
Twirling dancers with mismatched socks,
Create a rhythm, as time gently clocks!

Under the sun, no worries to bear,
We'll ride this wave, with sunshine to share.
Afternoon reveries bring such delight,
In the warmth of laughter, everything's right!

Golden Whispers

In the morning, I trip on a beam,
Chasing light like a silly dream.
Butterflies giggle, they dance and whirl,
Squirrels throw parties, what a crazy swirl!

Sunbeams tease me with a cheeky grin,
I tumble and tumble, let the fun begin.
A toast with lemonade, oh what a flair,
Laughter bubbles up, floats in the air!

The daisies in hats play hide-and-seek,
While ants are debating, who's the fastest or weak?
I wave to the clouds, "Hey, keep it bright!"
They wink at me, "We'll stay here all night!"

With every sip of the sweet lemonade,
I sprout new freckles, in sunshine cascade.
Life is a circus with squeals and cheer,
Golden whispers shine, nothing to fear.

Rays of Delight

A sunbeam slipped through my bedroom cracks,
Tickling my nose, I let out some quacks.
Wakey-wakey, the birds sing loud,
Join the parade, be part of the crowd!

I wear my sunglasses, though it's not that bright,
Giving a nod to the moon, what a sight!
The cat on the porch rolls over with glee,
"What a weird place, come join me!"

Jellybeans dance as I skip down the road,
Puddles giggle under my happy load.
Every leaf whispers, "Keep moving along,"
The sky hums with laughter, an old-time song.

With each step I take, the sunlight agrees,
It tickles my toes and fluffs up the breeze.
A parade of oddities, the day wears a crown,
With rays of delight, I'll never frown!

Sunkissed Melodies

In the meadow, the grass does a jig,
While fireflies waltz, in a luminous gig.
Fluffy clouds giggle, "We're just floating by!"
Lemonade waterfalls, oh my oh my!

The sun plays tricks, peekaboo all day,
My shadow's mischief—what will it say?
A watermelon slice does a somersault roll,
With each little bounce, it brightens the soul!

I dance with the daisies, in two left feet,
Stumbling and laughing, what a day to greet!
The bees buzz a tune, soft and sweet,
While ants start a conga, oh what a feat!

Sunkissed melodies swirl in the air,
With giggles and wobbles, I've no time to care.
The sun sets in giggles, it's time for a nap,
Dreams filled with laughter, a sunny cap!

Harvest of Warmth

The tomatoes in my garden wear hats of green,
While cucumbers joke, "We're the best you've seen!"
I pickle my worries in jars by the sun,
Summer's a party, let's all have fun!

Berries like confetti burst in my basket,
Chasing the rabbits, oh! What a task it!
Sunflowers wobble, trying to peek,
Whispering secrets—the flowers just squeak.

I sing to the pumpkins, my round little pals,
They roll for the laughter, avoiding the malls.
With honeycomb laughter and breezes so light,
We celebrate each day, oh what a delight!

The harvest of warmth wraps all around,
With twinkling giggles that dance on the ground.
So here's to the summer, the jokes that we share,
In the garden of laughter, I have not a care!

Sunlit Whispers

A cheeky sunbeam danced in my hair,
It tickled my nose with a glimmering glare.
I tried to catch it, oh what a chase,
But it giggled away with a warm embrace.

The clouds wore hats, oh what a sight,
They nodded their heads in pure delight.
I waved hello, they laughed in reply,
Who knew that clouds could be so spry?

The flowers chuckled, their petals aglow,
Telling secrets only the bees know.
I swear one blushed, as I strolled by,
Did a sunflower just wink? Oh my!

With every step, I felt so spry,
The world around me seemed to fly.
So here I am, beside this stream,
Chasing giggles, living the dream.

Warmth on My Skin

The sun, a prankster, on my skin lay,
Tickling toes in a silly ballet.
Each ray a joke, each glow a cheer,
Tans turn to laughter, it's perfectly clear.

Popsicles melting, drips down my chin,
A sweet disaster, where do I begin?
It's a sticky affair, laughter ensues,
As I scrub at the stains of my colorful hues.

Sunglasses perched, looking quite grand,
Reflecting my grin like a fun little band.
I waved to a squirrel, it waved back with glee,
This sunny day feels like a comedy spree!

So here's to the warmth, so bright and bold,
That sparks a giggle, a sight to behold.
Let's dance in the rays, let the laughter begin,
For every mishap, we're sure to win!

Laughter in the Breeze

Oh, how the wind carries giggles afar,
It whispers the secrets of a hidden bazaar.
Waving my hair in a playfully tease,
I chase after laughter that floats in the breeze.

A kite zoomed past, a colorful flop,
It tangled my thoughts, I couldn't quite stop.
The children below just erupted in cheers,
And I joined the chorus, dispelling my fears.

A warm gust blew by, a light-hearted jest,
It tickled my side, gave my senses a test.
'Stay on your toes,' said the playful wind,
As I twirled and I whirled, what a game to pretend!

So here we are, in this playful affair,
With laughter afoot, it dances in the air.
Let's join the breeze, be silly and free,
For joy is the secret we all need to see.

Sunkissed Memories

The beach ball was bouncing, oh what a show,
Each dive and splash put on smiles aglow.
I ran for the sandcastles, but oh what a sight,
A seagull swooped down and claimed it outright!

The ice cream truck jangled a sweet tune,
I chased it like a child, under the moon.
But one sticky scoop tumbled down to the ground,
And all that I heard was laughter abound.

With sun in my hair and sand on my feet,
I danced like a jester, so flaky, so sweet.
Each moment was silly, each memory bright,
Summer days filled with pure delight.

So let's gather these giggles, let's capture the sun,
Creating hilarious tales that can't be outdone.
For memories made under skies so divine,
Are the best kind of treasures, oh how they shine!

www.ingramcontent.com/pod-product-compliance
Lightning Source LLC
Chambersburg PA
CBHW070004300426
43661CB00141B/216